WATCHING BRIEF

Poems for the Journey

Michael Catling

Published by Wigmore Abbey Parish 2014

Copyright © Michael David Catling 2014

Text and illustrations are copyright and remain the property of the author. All rights reserved. No part of this book may be reproduced, stored in a retrieval system, or transmitted in any form or by any means (electronic, mechanical or otherwise) without prior permission in writing of the copyright holder.

First published September 2014 by
Wigmore Abbey Parish,
The Rectory, Dark Lane,
Leintwardine,
Craven Arms,
Herefordshire
SY7 0LJ.

A catalogue record of this book is available from the British Library.

ISBN 978-0-9930046-0-5

Set in 11pt Times New Roman.
Printed in England by Orphans Press Ltd., Arrow Close, Leominster Enterprise Park, Leominster, Herefordshire HR6 0LD.

The Poet enters into himself in order to create.
The contemplative enters into God in order to be created.

Thomas Merton
Seeds of Contemplation

FORWARD
by Henry Morgan

It is perhaps not surprising that there is a long tradition of Anglican priest-poets. Priesthood requires sensitive attention to the interface between humankind and God encompassed by creation, coupled with the felt need to articulate something of whatever is found therein. Most often the latter is delivered through a sermon within the setting of worship, but those who combine priestly calling with that of poet have other means at their disposal.

What may be more surprising is that this tradition is alive and well when there is much that militates against it. Most clergy are employed in urban areas and rural clergy like Mike frequently have many churches to look after. Today's Church is tempted to mimic the culture in which it stands, leading to a preoccupation with measureable results and a consequent driven need to be seen to be busy. That priestly men and women find the time and energy required to stand still and be attentive to the things of the Divine would seem unlikely, yet, clearly there are those who do.

There is a wonderful saying about the Church that 'it is like a swimming pool in that most of the noise comes from the shallow end'. A Church which is declining in number while interest in matters spiritual within society remains high, urgently needs voices from the deep end: and amongst those voices are poets like Mike.

I sense that more is being offered in this slim volume than might be immediately apparent. It is first and foremost a collection of poems arising from one priest's reflection on his calling. It deals with matters personal, pastoral and parochial, with his seeking after the God who called him and the occasions of his own encounters with that God. To read them is to be led into the work of spiritual awareness.

It is often said that the Anglican priest is called to 'the cure of souls' within his parish. These poems testify to Mike's vision of his own priestly calling as much to the soul of a place as to the souls within it: it is a calling to the whole of the created order. Although he grew up in London it has been the open spaces of Northumberland and, latterly, Herefordshire, which have nurtured this calling within him.

Implicit in these few poems is a vision of creation and one man's place in it under God that is not new but certainly uncommon in today's culture. It is a prophetic vision that prioritises the willingness to stand and stare; to wait upon what might be revealed, to exult in that revelation and to live with the emptiness when seemingly nothing is revealed. It's a vision that embraces doubt and not knowing as the only way to discover anything new. Without questions being asked, no answer will be forthcoming.

It is also a trumpet call to a particular vision of what priesthood is all about. It's not an easy vision nor is it one readily understood in our culture. It is of a priest being one who learns to lean both on his prayers and on a faith which is often stronger and more resilient than he feels it to be. It is a role that may feel a lonely one but the existence of the Sangha which has encouraged the publication of these poems suggests that there are those by whom it is valued.

The quotation from Thomas Merton speaks of the difference between the poet and the contemplative. Mike is a contemplative priest-poet who combines the attributes of both: he enters into God in order to be recreated, and into himself in order to create for the benefit of those he seeks, under God, to serve.

Henry Morgan June 2014

CONTENTS

Forward	4
Contents	6

* * * * * * * * *

The Poets	9
On Poetry Leaving	10
In Keats's Morning	12
Remembering R. S. Thomas	14
Weathered Prayer	17
If God was Green	19
Observation	21
Stigmata on the Heart	22
Hawthorn	23
Leaf Turning	24
Winter's Waning	25
Almost a Spring Morning	26
Noon	27
Evening Service at Duntrune	28
Boned Thoughts	29
Heron	30
Watching Brief	31
Thrush	32
Owl	33

Helmsman	34
Kite Spirit	35
Rainbow	36
Glasshampton Monastery Gardens	37
The Ruined Chapel	38
Waiting Room Revelation	39
Snapshot in a Wakefield Café	40
Mellerstain Portrait	41
The Conference	42
Journey's End is only the Beginning	44
Vestry Prayer	46
Confetti	47
Broken	48
The Priest's Apology	49
For Maureen	50
Parting	51
I have Painted God	52
Keeping Faith	53
Seeker	54
Heart's Flint	55
Silence	56
The Maze	57
Running the Race	58

The Hermit of Prayer	59
The Nativity Scene	60
The Word	61
On Reflection: Christ the Saviour	62
Man of Sorrows	63
The Buddha and the Christ	64
Free Fall	65
Soul Being	66
The Soul's Dust	67
Darkness Turning	68

* * * * * * * * *

Acknowledgements	71

The Poets

The poets scratch the meaning
    of love, truth and beauty
onto the granite heart of humanity;

but their marks do not go deep,
    and their words cannot withstand
the elemental forces of self-interest.

Standing on the promontory of communication,
    the sentences are not strong enough
to bridge the gap that has opened up

between the poet and those who construct
    knowledge rather than grow in wisdom.
The new millennium is already receding

into the conglomerate distance; and on the
    peninsula the language's vegetation decays,
leaving the poet terminally wordless and alone

on a now barren rock of hollow whispers
    where the utterances of faith echo back
from the darkness between the silent stars.

On Poetry Leaving

Faith, hope, and love, these three abide,
but not the poem and its poetry.
Repeatedly amorphous and translucent with meaning;
slipping through the mind's bars like fine sand
through childhood's fingers.
Intangible and only hauntingly reflected
in the soul's opaque mirror.

I know it now only in part,
but one day it will know me fully;
know who I am and am not.

Like the other three,
the poem and its poetry cannot be grasped
or held onto; disappearing through memory's
narrow gateway down the pathway of forgetting.

Open thought's palm and let it go,
this strange mystery that brings us always
to our beginning and our end,
teaching us of its indifference to birth and death.

In faith I have lived,
through hope I have trusted,
bearing love I have shared.

But the poem and its poetry
do not dwell for long,
only brushing the cheek
like a farewell kiss
on a cold morning
before turning and stepping
into the prose of the day.

In Keats's Morning

I have walked, more than once,
in Keats's morning of mellow
fruitfulness and seen the webs
stretched out like washing to dry;

noticed the wild flowers
bowing their small heads
under the weight of dawn's dew;
caught glimpses of sheep
moving like ghosts in the field's mist.

And I mentally balance these sights
like some kind of water boatman,
skimming languidly over the surface
of life's interior mirrored meaning,

partly enjoying the remission from
a season of untimely grey cold
and receiving the much needed
palliative care of yellow warmth
from the sun's restricted visiting hours.

But a fear remains that all
that troubles me may rise
to break the surface
in a final unprecedented storm

that cracks the light
and shatters the mellowness
to a jagged and broken melancholy,
driving Keats to a distant horizon,
as yet unnamed, as yet unfathomed…
                    in the distant skies.

Remembering R.S. Thomas

Introduced by his wife
he spoke no words,
simply offering a
perfunctory handshake;
his gaze following
his outstretched hand.

A gaze, emanating
from piercing eyes
that peered out of
a thinly papered face
on which was written
the lines of his wrestling

and his encounter
with Him who is who He is.
Then away to stare silently
at the flower bedecked font,
an offering from local schoolchildren,
remembering a mutual friend.

As if to enact his own poem,
he knelt to pray in the front pew;
this poet-priest kneeling before an
altar of wood in a stone church;
and there he stayed in silent stillness,
testing his embattled faith even now

waiting for the Absence
                          to speak
and declare its Presence
                          to an old man.

Poem inspired by a meeting with Mrs Frances Mason, who met R.S. Thomas briefly before a church service. The poet was then in his 80s.

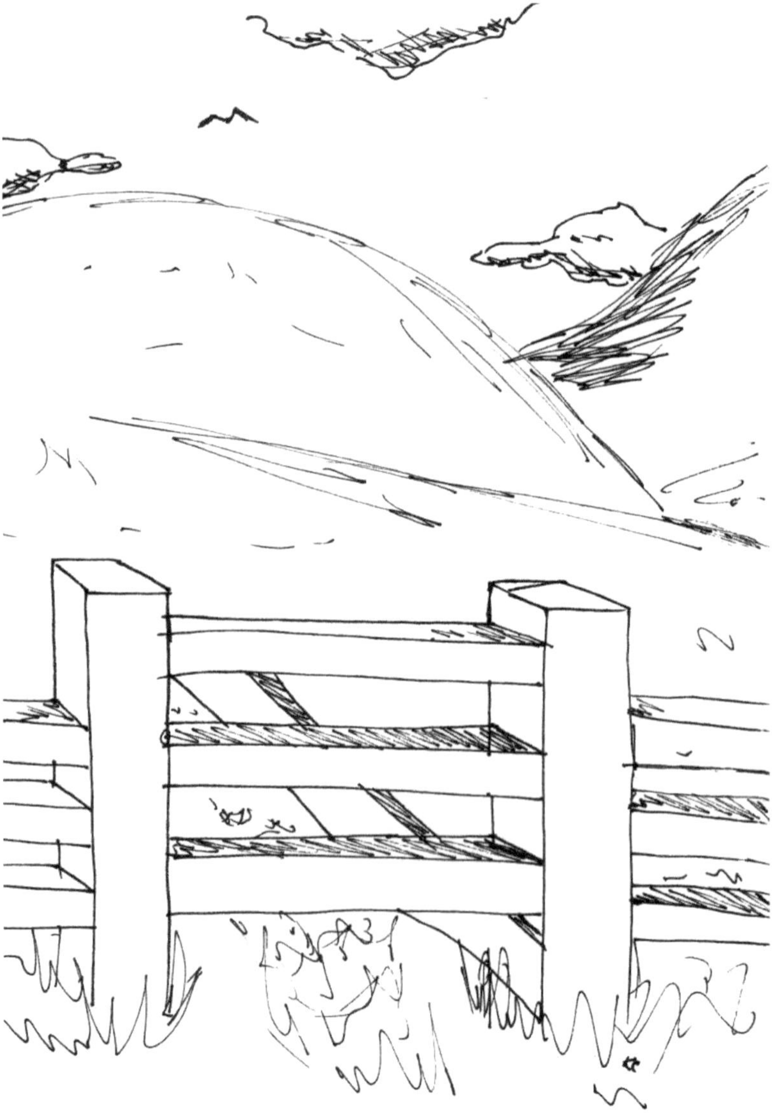

Weathered Prayer

The words are gusting,
being blown back in my face,
or if in a moment's calm
a phrase escapes beyond earshot
at the next rush it is scattered
like a flock of crows flying
headlong into the wind.

    * * * * * * * * * *

Words whither in the cold air
forcing the soul's dictionary
to close its covers against
a prevailing wind.
Prayer is a heron
flying gracefully close
to the earth's hardened surface.

    * * * * * * * * * *

Grey words on a grey background,
and lifting my eyes to the hills
I see only the cloud of unknowing
holding captive the vision.
Prayer returns slowly as a repeated
echo of my own thoughts before
settling on the muddied earth.

Prayer is an angel disappearing
into the warm air
unaware of its loss.
Becalmed silence and words drift
down as a single feather
to rest upon the earth.

     * * * * * * * * * *

Whitened words on a grey background;
lost on the page, but
transforming the landscape,
highlighting each rise and fall –
like prayer settling on life
with renewed meaning.

     * * * * * * * * * *

The words are cast like a shadow
across the earth by the prevenient
sun's rising. And somewhere the God
is startled into response
as grouse fly up from their resting
at the sound of footsteps in the field
walking in the cool of the morning.

If God was Green

If God was green
then the divine presence
would cover the fields
and climb the trees.
Alleluia!
All the shades of Godness
would be there for us to see.
We would clearly witness
green's fading and dying
at the winter season,
clearing the ground of being
for spring's resurrection
that comes forth
with the promise of new life
and new beginnings.
If God was green
how easy faith would be.
Yet instead we must look
intently for the green blade
rising within us out
of the soul's sacred soil.

Observation

Nature's palate resting in
the creases of the rock face,
shades mixed by clouds' gentle
touch and spread by sun's fingers
on ground's green-canvas outline.

Sheep, grey-white, move like
the clock's hand round the
field as if discerning the pattern
in the motion of time while,
mottled with steaming breath

and flicking tails, cattle stand
captive in the barn, bemoaning
the lack of day's fresh air in
which a pair of lapwings, fired
with fearful parental concern,

fly frantically in hope of drawing
my gaze away from the set-aside nest
tenanted in the open field and only
partially hidden by the dung hill,
bleached under the sun's interrogation.

Voices carry from a distant garden,
disembodied, but leaving their imprint
on the listener's mind; their presence
more permanent than the rotting manure,
discussing this green and pleasant land.

Stigmata on the Heart

The blossom is blown
    from the bough
        like pink tears
            from a cross

falling on those
    who can only
        stand and wait
            and look as

in gently fragile descent
    it alights upon the earth
        leaving an impress upon
            the weeping memory

and a stigmata etched
upon the sacred heart
    reminding us where
        love has been and

yet will come again.

Hawthorn

Hawthorn,
    bare and gaunt but
for a few leaves
    hanging, declaring
life in the midst
    of arboreal death.

You stand
    as if re-rooted from
a blasted heath
    scratching post
for sheep whose
    grey woollen strands

clinging to your
    splintered bark
serve as a poor
    shroud in the hour
you are hewn
    from earth's embrace.

Mindborn,
    you are leaning like
a schoolmaster over
    a disobedient pupil
exacting punishment
    for a childish prank

that unknowingly brings
    about your demise.

Leaf Turning

Is each leaf counted,
like hairs on the head,
as its grasp slips from the tree?

Is there perhaps a pre-ordained
place to which it is blown?
Or does it whirl and twist

in freefall, randomly landing
unannounced on the now
frigid skin of the cooling earth?

And for every spiralling, dying leaf
does God in supra-luminous darkness
breathe upon a barren tree

or turn over a new leaf, ready
for another virginal spring and
promise of fecund hope to come?

And am I blown randomly
in endless freefall or is there
a place for which I am bound?

And how many new leaves
must I turn over before
arriving at another greening spring.

Winter's Waning

The greying snow
is receding on
the landscape's hairline,
hiding in the crevices
of ancient field systems,
(exposed by winter's sun),
crouching against hedges and walls,
planted and built by men
now resting beneath the earth
they once broke skin and hearts
on generations ago.

Soon it will be spring again.
Snow and the soil's midwives
will slip deeper into memory's
recesses, recounting irrelevances.

Almost a Spring Morning

Reading Thomas for breakfast -
digesting the roughage of his words
along with the muesli -
before walking the greening fields
hoping to green the mind
after the brown dirge of winter.

Listening to the burn's banter
answering the wind's sigh,
I hear the cry of the buzzard,
like a petitioner's prayer,
soaring above the mind's babble
of life's perennial questions.

I walk on,
in search of the great silence
that language cannot penetrate
or shatter.

Noon

The space beyond the open door
                      is filled with
wind sound
           bird song
                      insect susurration

like mind's thoughts
                ricocheting off the bone
boundary of the skull
                into memory's vaults.

Church clock striking noon
                echoes the reminder
that one cannot take
                time out of time

but only continue travelling
                round the face
that will bring the orbiting poet
                back to a beginning again

in the hope of recognising his
                      features in a mirrored soul
deeply hidden
                by the reflection of
                      its own making.

Evening Service at Duntrune

Evening prayer with bird-psalm antiphons,
sacred readings from nature's congregation
gathered within the walls of green hills
and ceiling of blue sky
blessed by white fingered clouds
reflected on the floor of calm waters.

The wind whispers wisdom
into my listening soul
acting as this dusk's Magnificat,
whilst Simeon's Song laps against
the shore's heart, eternally
ebbing and flowing like light and darkness
across the loch's silent surface
making this son of man gloriously insignificant
yet touched by grace and filled by love
in at-one-ment with the fellowship of all creation
residing in the breath of the Creator.

Boned Thoughts

Skeletal thoughts …
    like winter's trees,
    darkened and blackened
    by persistent rain;
    drooping branches as
    sentinels of the dark burn
    babbling through
    ancient gnarled roots,
    keeping conversations,
    washing over memories
    and 'only ifs' …

suspended by the heron's
decaying corpse
lying on a mulched bier.
    Now the breeze recites
    the song of lamentation
    grieving this loss of
    miraculous simplicity.

Thoughts and the heron
merge into wingless flight.

Heron

The dark, blue-grey presence
stands silent and motionless on the riverbed
as the flow of shallow water
offers its continued blessing.

Its bill is poised, eyes alert,
ready to make its darting and precision grip
upon the unsuspecting and slippery
body of the fish passing below its shadow.

This living metaphor of nature's quiescent
contemplative at prayer, who sits
in the flowing presence of the holy,
mind and heart moving out beyond

the shallows of existence,
poised to feed on the slippery instant
of enlightenment and awakening,
bringing blessing to mind's eye and heart's care.

Watching Brief

An audience of swallows,
perched on the five-bar garden fence,
sit staring it seems
through my study window
watching me at work.

Their conversation is constant
and familiarly frenetic
as if passing continual comment
on my posture, my looks, or my work-rate.
And then, like a gust of wind

scattering fallen autumnal leaves,
they disappear into the sky,
leaving an image of their feathered presence,
and a silence, interrupted only
by the hum of the computer.

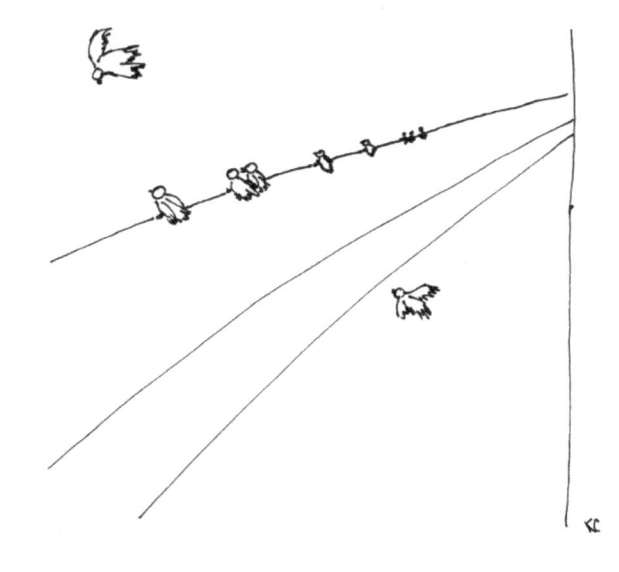

Thrush

I saw God this morning.
He was perched on a fencepost
close to the road.

His speckled breast
on full view,
unlike Elijah's hidden theophany.

His head was turned
so that one small eye
could take all of me in.

It was as if he looked
into the depths of my soul,
searching for an affinity.

We both stood
for just a few moments
in each other's presence.

We acknowledged
the sense of knowing
and being known.

It was I who moved first,
walking away down the road,
assured that I would not be alone.

Owl

I heard the owl call,
much like God does,
distant and unseen.
Tempted as I am
to leave the well-
trodden path in twilight,
I know he will remain
elusive, hidden, calling
always from one tree
further into the distance
as I seek to approach.
Looking down at me as
I cannot look up at him.

The Helmsman

With just a single, horizontal row of feathers,
on the very margin of the forked tail,
these kites soar above me with angled wings.

Buoyant, as the tall ships I once saw out beyond the Tyne,
each one is a helmsman of the sky, breaking and steering
in fearless flight like angels declaring good news upon earth.

These fine feathers, granting graceful, imaginative manoeuvres
are known ironically as the 'rector's feathers', who, in human
 form,
is a far cry (not unlike the kite's) from any sense of direction.

Feeling flightless, like a fallen angel, no longer at the helm,
rudderless in the sacred space with his crew,
he sails in and towards the mystery that is God.

A reality that is like the great ocean beyond us, all around us,
(and within us), but if his tide ebbs today, as one priest
has already remarked, it will flow full tomorrow.

Kite Spirit

Overhead, the majestic kite
circling as I imagine
the Spirit did over
the turbulent waters.

Overheard, the lofty kite's
mewing as I imagine
God's voice might summon
me to life in abundance.

Overwhelmed by this creature's
elevated flight and inspiring call,
I respond, rising up on the Spirit's
thermal presence out of chaos.

Rainbow

        So close,

you could touch it;

        if not

with outspread fingers

        then, perhaps,

with unfurled mind.

        It brings

to remembrance the

        ethereal promise

that God will not flood

        the senses

with his transparent presence.

        Rather by

coloured reflection, refraction,

        and dispersion,

he will arch over

        the one tree

left standing vacant,

        imaging the

untenanted cross of our faith.

Glasshampton Monastery Garden
'God is a singing sound in the heart of silence'

Silence here seeps into my soul
Like a plant absorbing water through its roots.
As a scent inhaled from the flower blooms,
God comes to me through the still air.

Silence caresses me like a gentle kiss
upon the cheek, an acknowledged presence
like the arrival of the breeze on a sultry summer's day,
the lightest touch of reassurance on the shoulder.

And with this silence the soul's ear cupped
to enjoy the symphony of silent music.
The sounding of solitude in the deep fathoms
of the heart, not unlike the buzz of contented bees

around the chimney stack in this garden of tranquillity
where the singing sound of God reverberates
like the voices of the brothers chanting their prayers
through the rhythm of another perfect day.

The Ruined Chapel

The unforgiving salt wind blows
through the eyeless windows
and up and out of this roofless chapel.
Sailors and saints once gave thanks
for safe passage to the shore below;
now the only offering is the relentless
cries of circling gulls.

A few stones remain upon others
like faith's memorial to a forgotten
lover, one whose intimacy
was rejected by fickle passion.
So we stand within the remains
of belief stretched out in prayer
like torn sails upon the rocks below,
rudderless without repentance.

Our learnéd words build but
a hollow tower unfurnished.
Unlike the gulls our flight is
wingless and our endless cries
are left marooned on the shore.
The ebb and flow of your presence
teases out the soul from its shell.

Waiting Room Revelation

Sitting in the waiting room,
the cat in the box complaining
about the décor and the lack of space,
when, unannounced, the sun peers
through the window casting
the shadow of a cross with its frame
across the space between myself
and the flustered receptionist's desk.
My head is silhouetted on the left arm
of the cross, whilst my mind is thinking:
'How strange to see a cross on the floor
of the waiting room in the vet's surgery.
                        Should I pray?'

Then a lady, called Mary, enters the surgery,
a light brown mongrel walking
sprightly on the end of a dark brown lead.
'He doesn't look in need of treatment.'
I say to myself, as Mary and dog
report their presence to the receptionist,
who is expressing to all the fact that
this is not one of her better days.
Then Mary sits on a chair diagonally
opposite, so that her attentive pet
sits in the middle of the cross
cast by the sun on the floor of
                        the waiting room.

Then I understand the revelation
that has just taken place before my eyes:
Dog on the cross.

Snapshot in a Wakefield Café

The old man, leather-faced,
sits in the corner of the café.
His eyes, like his dinner plate,
are empty, remembering what
has been and is no more.

The waitress, tight-jeaned,
young enough to be his daughter,
walks across from behind the counter
carrying a nondescript pudding
buried in custard to his solitary table.

Placing bowl and spoon in front of him,
she leans down close and puts an arm
around the shoulder of his ragged raincoat.
Whispering words into his ear
the leathered face becomes momentarily supple.

The empty eyes fill with perhaps
a moment's memory of other women's whispered words.
A smile is released from the creases of his face,
his body relaxes into the woman's embrace
and the years fall tumbling from his body.

The moment passes as the waitress
walks away to serve another customer,
but the old man smiles on for a few seconds more
before turning his gaze on his pudding
and lifting the tarnished spoon to his lips,
becoming lost in the menu that life has left him.

Mellerstain Portrait

And if you stepped from your frame
what would you be …
seductive, sensuous, or solicitous?

And if your eyes acknowledged me
how would we be …
calculating, casual, or conspiratorial?

And if you chose to speak my name
what words would there then be …
welcoming, wistful, or withering?

And if our meeting inveigled us
how would it look to be …
between biased bystanders,

the pair of us framed
by the time between us …
lamenting, longing and lost?

An imagined conversation with Lady Grisell Bailie encountered at Mellerstain House in the Scottish Borders

The Conference
Day One

The words ebbed and flowed,
wetting the bottom of the rolled up
trousers of my intellect (to begin with).
Then they washed over me,
pounding my brain and drowning out
their meaning as they crashed, crashed,
against the shifting sands of my mind.

Every castle of understanding
was washed away without trace.
Every footprint of the journey
erased, as if it had never existed.
A fluid welcome to the shoreline, then,
newly created and marked by a seaweed of
language, bladderwrack thoughts popping

at the warmth of a question to which
there is no answer other than the seagull's cry,
as it turns over the empty shell of faith.

Day Two

Added the scaffolding of my words
to the tower under construction
already well on the way to heaven
and expanding outwards towards
the four corners of a round earth.

Welcomed onto the construction site
by fellow builders, I laboured hard
through the long hours of the day
in an effort to complete the task
of reaching the boundaries we saw,

only to find that the God we were
climbing towards declared there was
none.

Journey's End is Only the Beginning
Aachen Cathedral

Did Charlemagne know that one day
I would arrive at his palace chapel
as a tourist and leave as a pilgrim?

On entering this ancient sacred space
was it his hand held out in welcome
to one weary from the journey?

Was it his voice that uttered those familiar
words of blessing first spoken at the dawn of time,
'Behold, it is very good!'?

Did he guide me to sit before Mary and her child
in order to hear the echoes of a previous conversation
returning from somewhere deep within?

'Come and be one who blesses souls in my son's name'.

With these words came a peace
in which I was held and remembered
by one 'younger than the life in me.'

Perhaps he knew what I did not know
and that is sometimes best, but not to know
of knowing is a disease and now healing came.

I did not know I had been lost
but was now found again, gathered in
from the briars of expectations and demands.

'Gather up the sheaves of your vocation
and leave rejoicing in remembrance of me.
Trust the balance of calm and chaos, faith and fear.

Learn to be both Mary and Martha,
active in stillness and at peace in activity.'
With these words Charlemagne and I parted.

He carried my gratitude and I put on his blessing.

Vestry Prayer

I wait in this vestry
for God to arrive before
morning worship begins,
standing motionless amongst
the bric-a-brac that passes
as life in this sacred space,
only to realise it mirrors
the accumulated jumble
that passes for faith in
the dust of the heart's warehouse.

If the meaning is in the waiting,
then this morning enlightenment
does not come, and, if present,
God hides in the dark recesses,
unnoticed, and the Christ-light
fails to tease him out into the open.

Confetti

Here, in the parish, they ask still:
'Do I like being here?'
'Have I settled in yet?'
'Will I be staying?'

I reply that
even though the marriage celebration
is slowly beginning to fade from memory
and the honeymoon is all but over,
there are still the frequent and well aimed
showers of confetti.
Enough for me to keep my vows
to this place and its people,
for better, for worse, in sickness and in health.

Enough even to believe
that between the mud and the breath of God,
together, we can discover
the ordinariness of our shared humanity.

Broken

The wind breaks against the slate church roof
as the priest breaks the wafer over the silver chalice.

Rafters rattling in protest dislodge stone dust
as crumbs fall into the blood-red liquid.

Both fall silently, unnoticed by the faithful few
gathered to share in word and sacrament.

The stone dust falls onto the bowed heads
while discoloured wafer crumbs float on the surface.

Worshippers carry the dust to the communion rail
and return having imbibed the crumbs of the presence.

Does God come this silently into our midst
showering his blessing like dust upon the prayerful?

Do those kneeling with a whispered 'amen'
swallow the Christ who came to save them?

Do earthly dust and sacramental crumbs, one uninvited
the other taken by choice, combine to reveal his oneness?

Wind and priest, stone dust and wafer crumb,
joining as conduits of a fine and broken God,

bestowing on those with dust in their veins and
the unworthiness of crumbs from life's table

a quiet faith in anticipation of a greater feast.

The Priest's Apology

No, I cannot call you
out of the tomb's darkness
that clasps you to the cold
stone of its heart.

Nor can I still
the storm that wreaks
havoc on your once
calm and sheltered shore.

I have sought to bind
the wound that will not
heal, to feed the hungry soul
and water the thirsty spirit.

But all I have are the stories
of one who reportedly did,
once, and an empty book
whose words defy meaning;

its liturgical language lost,
alongside my pallid prayers.
I am Christ's peasant
set to work in the fields

sowing seeds that time only
will know of their germination;
pushing through the darkened earth
in search of daylight in furrowed souls.

For Maureen

Gone now . . . ?

Without trace,
No more you,
In a familiar place.

Just a void, a gap, an emptiness;
Only a photo or two
Left in remembrance.

Together again,
Just belatedly, briefly, brilliantly;
And now only this pain.

Always my sister, but in *absentia*;

. . . Or now brought together
Transfiguring time and space,
Held in memory's forever.

Sorrow now, but not decay,
Transition maybe, not death.
                      Eternal now, not trapped in yesterday.

Parting . . .

I'll sing this one last lullaby
which you will hear but
not be able to respond to.
The journey of no return has begun,
the darkness fading as you travel
towards the illumination of self,
mirrored in the welcoming smile of God.

The hum of words to a plain tune
bring together both birth and death.
Vulnerable and speechless you came,
likewise, you now take your leave.
On arrival, pray for us now
and in the hours of our need.
In your weakness be our strength.

Drifting deeper into the final sleep
as the voice of one singing
caresses wasted body and waiting soul
in words of lament and farewell.
Travelling to a distant shore,
don't forget to send back word
that all is well and all shall be well.

I Have Painted God

I have painted God
        with such broad brushstrokes
that it has become
        difficult to decipher him from
the colour of the canvas.

His presence has faded
        from vermilion's blood-red
to pastel shades hardly
        visible in the shadow of
a watered-down faith.

The perspective changes
        almost daily from linear
pathways to circular tracks;
        finding myself like Milne's
bear, covering ground I have

already trod in search of an
        answer not hiding in branches,
but buried in the roots
        of a soul waiting to find
a welcoming dawn's daylight.

Keeping Faith

I keep my faith
in an intricately decorated enamelled box
on the table beside my bed.

And when night's darkness
penetrates even the closed eyelids,
or morning's lethargy
leaves me cocooned in the duvet,
I reach out and lift my faith
gently from its box
and nurse it close to my heart,
listening for its breath of comfort.

Thus I keep the faith, my faith,
hidden, sheltered and protected,
safely in this room away from those
whose questions infect it with doubt's virus.

Yet . . .
each time of the lid's lifting
I notice my faith has grown frailer still,
its heartbeat harder to monitor, until
I fear that the box will become its shrine.

Seeker

So, you are a seeker
        in search of the word?
                Beware!

I have seen such
        caught and torn on
the barbed wire of
              silence

when no word came
        as they advanced from
their entrenched positions.

Visiting them in the
        infirmary I see them,
              staring

past me at God's breath
        condensing
on life's mirror.

The Heart's Flint

To journey across
the imagined boundary
requires the ready heart;
striking its flint
with the steel of truth,
igniting the spark
that lights life's tinder
and gives birth
to the living flame.
Blow, Spirit, blow
on the embers of
faith and hope
and watch them
glow into being.

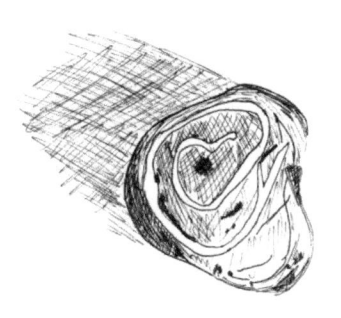

Silence

I know your silence,
reminiscent of speechless echoes
running through the windowless
corridors of faith or
falling softly as scented
petals on the hardwood floor
of my impermanent dwelling.

Almost always audible,
like the bat's signal on midsummer's night.
Yet the straining ears and searching eyes
miss again the sound of your passing
and the fleeting image we were
created from in the beginning.

The Maze

I pursue you as in a maze;
hearing the sound of your
footsteps ahead of me, and
following them, turn the corner
to see only the fading footprints
of one who has already
disappeared from view.

So this game of hide and seek
continues, until reaching
the centre and knowing
that you are cornered,
I turn and come face to face
with the transparent physiognomy
of the one known as 'God'.

Running the Race

'Are you an athlete?' she asked.
'No not really.' I replied.
'I'm only an athlete of the mind,
running endlessly
around the track of my thoughts.'

'Do you never finish?' she queried.
'My predecessor ran to win the prize,
competitive to the last. I find that in ending
a new thought is already
under starter's orders'.

The Hermit of Prayer

Stalking the hermit of prayer
I followed him into the barren desert,
sand and grit erasing the skin from my feet
lodging in the orifices of my body
and matted in my hair.
I came upon him suddenly
kneeling like an ancient boulder
in the landscape head tilted heavenwards,
eyes fixed on the invisibly eternal presence
to which he offers all that he has and all that he is.

Many years before I heard the folk duo sing,
'every heart needs a home.'
Now those words echoed
through my soul's cage
like one crying in the wilderness,
'Can you make *my* paths straight?'
And the voice of the bearded Coptic bishop,
robed in black from head to foot,
inviting me to take 'a piece of the desert'
home so that a busied heart
might rest in the still solitude
imaged now in the hermit's offering.

The Nativity Scene

The birth that threads its way
through the woven cloth of life
with the cry of new born being that
echoes through the surface sounds
of sorrow and sighing -
so much 'our daily bread' -
is close at hand, poised as if
in the wings awaiting its entrance
onto the stage where audience
and actors together merge into
a nativity of their own making
in which blood, and sweat, and tears
are air-brushed out to leave
a domestic scene of bliss by starlight;
creatures and humanity gathered
with welcoming breath and doleful eyes.

So be it! But, as the poet once wrote,
this birth invites our death into
the rising of life itself within.
A looking beyond the mirrored
image of our own reflection
to catch a glimpse of the one
who repeatedly declares the 'I am'
in the steady beat of the heart's manger.

The Word

The Holy Calligrapher raises the pen to inscribe
the Word upon the heart's parchment.
Not the email or text that, like heaven and earth,
will be deleted and pass away.

In a corner of life's library, surrounded by the autobiographies
of Word bearers, the reader's concentrated gaze sheds
light on its meaning, sitting resting in the silent stillness
that balances the enquiring mind with the discerning heart.

Turning the emotion's page, I read that
it is better to journey than to arrive.
Reaching the destination means there is nowhere else to go,
 but only to stand stationary on the decaying platform of religion's
dogma.

Believing we possess the truth we do not seek it,
forgetting that knowledge is transient; its offering is only cairns
for the journey that is both linear and cyclical; we return
only to leave under the direction of the heart's compass.

The Holy Calligrapher sets down the pen,
the sentence finished. The Word is etched upon
the heart's parchment, the ink drying at the spirit's comma.
The signature is permanent unlike the finger's inscription in the
sand.

On Reflection: Christ the Saviour
A response to Andrei Rublev's icon

I'm looking at this battered, wooden Christ
who's been trodden underfoot and walked on
by countless foreign boots, lying as a floorboard
in a woodshed out beyond the town.

Your face and body scratched, the paint flaking off,
damaged by years of ignorance and neglect.
Yet still you turn towards me, conscious of my need,
a gaze full of compassion without trace of condemnation
for one who tried to turn stones into bread.

Such tenderness in suffering only splinters the wrecked soul I
                                            have become.
A heart that is downtrodden even though I once walked the extra
                                                          mile.
Now I'm standing on the secret I've forgotten long ago
in this shed without a window and walls without a door.

You'll observe my looks and physique
have been scratched and damaged by years of regret
but I see you reaching out with those broken fingers
to my suffering within. Your eyes penetrate my darkness
with a light that won't give in.

If we both get off this floor then I promise
we'll make it hand in hand to a place
where the wind blows and the river can't be dammed.
Then we'll sit and surrender to the prayer that flows within.

Man of Sorrows

The wilderness blog,
dry, barren, words turning
to dust on the tongue,
images without metaphor,
shadowless in meaning.
Windstorm in the soul
and out beyond the mind's horizon
rising as the sand's tide
to blow him away
– sightless –
or to suck him in
– breathless –
thus speaks this (or any)
man of sorrows,
head bent, knees to chest,
spirit foetal-shaped, anticipating
death by forsakenness,
the cord of love severed
from its source,
crying out in echoes from the soul's cavern,
'Let this pass so I remain if not by my will then by yours.'

And from within the smouldering bush
the hidden presence,
the keeper of shadows,
the desert dweller,
blinks back a tear
as the rose might retract to its bud
or the spoken word become a whisper
lost in the sound of silence.

The Buddha & The Christ

The Buddha and the Christ
sitting at my heart's table.
One serene and smiling,
the other troubled and weary.

They share sacred silence
and break bread together,
companions orbiting in
the reality of my being.

The Christ declares, 'I am.'
The Buddha replies, 'I am not.'
Is this still the question:
'To be or not to be?'

Or maybe not to be two
but only to be the one.
Two faces, yet one heart
beating with love's compassion.

Free-fall

I am ready for the letting go,
the jumping without being pushed.
The leaping from the mind's cliff
edge into free-fall, spinning down
into the deep but dazzling darkness
of faith, falling into the abyss
of the naked now, stripped bare
of believing that I know,
but trusting that I am known.

The wind's rush,
the spirit's whisper,
endlessly repeating
the promise of presence.
At last the soul's mantra
like prayer flags in brittle air
finds communion descending
into wholly sacred space;
and the ground of being broken
open to receive this prodigal
with celebration and embrace.

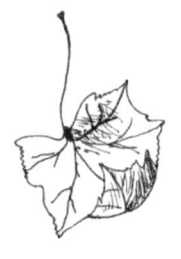

Soul-being

To know …
    I am the *SPACE*
        between the words
            on the page.

To know …
I am the *PAUSE*
    at the end of
        the spoken word.

To know …
I am the *SUNLIGHT*
    shining through
        the wood's canopy.

To know …
    I am the *SEED*
        carried by the wind to
            the fertile earth.

To know …
    I am the *SILENCE*
        after the cessation
            of the cacophony.

To know …
    I am the *SIGH*
        at the end of
            the painful ordeal –

is to know
    divine breath caressing
        the soul of my being
            into abundant life.

The Soul's Dust

The questioning wind
blows the soul's dust
into the mind's air,

whilst leaves fidget
like the fingers on
an anxious hand – waiting

for room in sanctuary's space,
a stilling in the storm's eye,
respite from fury's disbelief.

Beyond imagination's rail
clouds beat a retreat
across the militant sky.

Sunlight and shadows dance
like faith and doubt entwined
to a discordant, polyphonic tune;

bending grasses appearing
to bow to an unseen master
mouthing words unheard.

And after the wind
the dust comes to rest
briefly on departing souls.

Darkness Turning

In the sometime fading light of trembling faith,
when night seems to squirrel into the corners of my soul,
friend's words echo through the hollow halls of memory.
Once again I am in the darkness clasping the unseen.
It is then that rational speech becomes unsayable
and silence slips its arms round my helplessly hoping heart.
My wordless prayer reaches out for the Christ-light
in the hope of it casting shadows on the blank
walls of my trusting that darkness turning brings light.
In the glimmer of the flame flickering fearlessly
I see a glimpse of the unseen both held and holding me
through the cycles of this so soon lived life,
and as I gather so am I gathered in embrace
expectant that tomorrow's dawn brings sight.

ACKNOWLEDGEMENTS

This book of poems would never have come into being without the encouragement and support of others.

Firstly humble thanks to Annette, Carole, Sue and members of the Sangha whose initial enthusiasm spurred on the whole project; to Sir Lesley Fielding for supporting and believing in the book from the outset; to all those who have read the poems in parish magazines throughout the years and given such positive comments on their contents.

In addition my thanks go to Jo, my wife, who painstakingly edited and formatted the material for this book, and to my daughter, Katie, whose delightful illustrations enhance the collection; to Henry Morgan, my Spiritual Director and friend, for his introduction that reveals how well he dares to know me; to Jane Wells for the cover design that captures the spirit of the book so well.

Grateful thanks are due to those whose generous donations have made publication possible and to Orphans Press for their genuine enthusiasm and advice.

Finally, I wish to acknowledge my indebtedness to R.S. Thomas, poet-priest, whose poetry remains a challenging inspiration on my spiritual journey.